# Mindfulnes Multitasking

## A Plea for a More Conscious Life

*"What day is it?" asked Winnie the Pooh*
*"It's today!", squeaked Piglet*
*"Oh, I'm so glad, as today is my favorite day.", said Pooh.*

Life in the Here & Now

© 2015, Madame Missou
2. Edition, October 2015
ISBN-13: 978-1495376498
ISBN-10: 1495376494
Madame Missou is represented by
Maracuja GmbH, Laerheider Weg 13
47669 Wachtendonk, Germany
info@madamemissou.de
www.madamemissou.de

# Table of contents

# 1. Introduction

*Bonjour mes amis!*

Time is precious. The time in our life is limited. Our working hours can't be extended at will, and neither can our leisure time. Thus we try to optimize the use of our hours. We want to achieve, experience and organize as much as possible - and as quickly as possible.

However, do we really take advantage of the available time by cramming it and trying to do too many things at once?

Increasingly complex tasks and requirements at work, more and more offers for leisure time, and continuously more possibilities of material, medial-related, and intellectual consumption tempts many of us. Inevitably, we overburden ourselves. Be it in the professional field or in private situations, in nearly all parts of life we practice multitasking or at least we try to, often even without noticing it, regardless of gender!

Is this lifestyle healthy? Does it lead it anywhere, can it create satisfaction in the long run and what effect does it have on our relationships? And there are more questions like these: what is the reason? Why is multitasking becoming so prevalent in my lifestyle? Is it a lack of self-regard? Too little of my own standing? Or the urge of trying to be perfect and to satisfy everyone?

Or is multitasking, or rather the lifestyle to overburden oneself, a welcome distraction from certain aspects of my life and a way of avoiding them?

We can't increase the time that we have in our lives. We can only use it intensively and in the present. This guidebook promotes a careful handling of oneself and of others. Not only that. It provides practical insights into the dangers of multitasking and gives suggestions for a more considerate and livable lifestyle. While you are reading you will have the chance to actively look at the matter that is your life and to make surprising discoveries. You will gain thought-provoking impulses for the areas in which you might be able to become more successful, life quality and easiness with the help of mindfulness. Whether in your career, your family, or in a relationship, a lifestyle based on mindfulness is beneficial - especially for you.

It goes without saying that this little guide can't entirely fathom the whole aspect of mindfulness in 45 minutes of reading. Therefore, consider this book a helpful introduction and inspiration for everyone, who wants to know more but doesn't know where to start. Some tips and tricks may seem familiar to you. Some will certainly be new. Pick up whatever is important to you - or, in the best case, whatever touches you and start to build on that. Also, if you realize in some areas that something inside you starts to move and the desire for it increases, then further explore in advanced literature, coaching, seminaries or simply in good conversations with friends.

All I can do now is to wish you fun and "success" while reading this book stress-free. Remove yourself from the rest of the world so that you can enjoy this book in silence and without distraction. I've given you so much already for the first 45 minute-mindfulness-exercise! This will actually begin for you in chapter two.

*Bisous,*
*Madame Missou*

## 2. Multitasking as a Lifestyle - Prospects and Problems

### 2.1 Multitasking - Desirable, Fascinating, Unnecessary, or Harmful?

In many areas, the ability to multitask is considered a desirable. (S)he who is capable of quickly adapting to different people and various requirements seems dynamic and eloquent. As our society becomes more and more complex, the importance of networking is on the rise. People that can multitask fulfill important tasks in key positions. In their everyday life, physicians and mothers, assistants and team leaders all can't help but focus on numerous matters and tasks and settle them as perfectly as possible. Who can manage all that authority does a good job, and that is the general social consensus. Nevertheless, is it actually possible to juggle so many things at once with autonomy or is it a common, grand illusion that harms all of us?

### 2.2 Where Does the Term "Multitasking" Come From?

The idea of multitasking derives from the field of information technology. The term describes the ability of operation systems to continuously interrupt processes and to restart them shortly after. Since processes are interrupted and restarted in short intervals, the impression of simultaneousness appears. The reason consists in making use of times, in which the processor is waiting for external results. The goal is a maximum use of resources.

Already at this point we are indeed to question if a model from the world of information technology is suitable as a model for our own life.

## 2.3 Feeling Vivacity

Whoever experiences elation of an energetic, mental state, perceives a temporary dynamism, which is perceived as enjoyable on different levels. Feeling competent, spontaneous, accessible at any time as well as productive is fun. There are situations in which we make use of multitasking with great pleasure and it gives us great energy. This feeling is exactly the opposite of boredom. It can be joyful, it gives certainty that we are needed and that we are at the right place at the moment. It confirms one of our most important basic needs. We feel self-efficacy on a high scale.

Multitasking can therefore very well be healthy and beneficial. But this is in the right dosage. Like almost all things in our lives, it can fulfill its purpose and make our life more interesting, richer and more colorful.

## 2.4 Why is Multitasking so Dangerous?

It is my personal opinion that whoever has incorporated too many multitasking elements into their life is living dangerously. We have gotten used to the notion that many activities ought to happen almost simultaneously or subsequently. Consequently, we often don't even realize how we overburden ourselves and how we steamroll others. This is because we have internalized multitasking so strongly. The ability of doing different activities subsequently or supposedly concurrently, even having many different thoughts while doing so and keeping an overview of all the things around us is being admired and highly praised. The question is: for whom is it useful? Is it good for myself, or is it especially useful for others? And also: is it really useful to others, or does the whole thing have a bitter downside anyway? Are we losing a sense for the essential?

*Example:*

You are heading a difficult meeting for the first time and after a successful reception, you get to the first point on the agenda. You are prepared well and you feel comfortable. It is important to you, however, to gain the attention of the attendees from the start. With great satisfaction you notice that you have got the whole audience focused on you and your words. Everybody is listening with excitement. Suddenly, one of your colleagues is already starting to hand out fliers through small talk. It is swishing, and all the attendees are starting to check out the heap of apparently important documents that are being passed on. The concentration has vanished. You are probably experienced enough to get the attention of your audience again. Yet perhaps your colleague has disturbed with her well-intended action and taken away important energy from you.

Perhaps you know similar situations from your job, your family or your charity boards. If you can and want to place yourself into these situations, we invite you to answer some of the following questions:

- Would you have considered the flyer-act a disturbance, or completely normal?
- How would you feel in that situation?
- Was the act really necessary, or would it have been enough to pass the fliers around at a later stage?
- Would you talk to your colleague about the situation and ask her to wait for a break next time?

It is possible that you have not ever found yourself in a similar situation. Perhaps you are so trained and independent that you are not at all vulnerable to disruptions. Still, perhaps you would have preferred and found it more professional to keep the attention of the listeners. This very trivial example is one of many little events we encounter throughout the day. We are unnecessarily disrupted by a goal-oriented action. The number of times we disturb others in the same way is incredibly high. As a group or society, isn't there a better way of dealing with things?

We need to have a change of lifestyle. We need to be more aware of ourselves and of others. We shouldn't ask ourselves primarily, what could - at that very moment - still happen from an economic point of view but rather **what is important in every moment** and what requires our full attention. I believe that that's the core of the matter.

## 2.5 Brain Researches Confirm: Multitasking Steals Energy

We want to save time and energy and we want to execute our activities as efficiently as possible. However in doing so, we attract energy killers. If we want to deal with many things at once, we indulge ourselves in the fantasy that handling tasks subsequently or simultaneously is actually possible.

When we are trying to multitask, we fail to take into account that we always have to try and understand completely different issues. By jumping from one job to the next, we keep on making our life more difficult than is necessary. It means that we are constantly and unnecessarily straining our brain with many very different, often opposing demands. The effect is fatal, according to brain research findings. We manage our tasks worse than if we had handled them one by one.

Far too often we believe that when everything is happening at the same time, we are working at peak efficiency. The opposite holds true however. We actually become more vulnerable to disruption and hence work more slowly. We think way too often that multitasking and hectic living are necessary. Yet this is far less frequently the case than we believe. A great example is doctors on call and paramedics. Their work is life saving but they still work harmoniously in a structured fashion, completing one task before starting the next. They prioritize specific tasks and are not working on three emergencies simultaneously.

## 2.6 Self-consciousness and Self-esteem Diminish

How do you see yourself? Do you want to be a person who can operate in all directions, being ready for anything at any time? Or would you rather be someone who can set priorities and who settles everything stress-free one by one and who can sort out daily tasks according to their importance? Whoever allows themselves to be swamped over by requests, which are all the most important, and in doing so, settles matters with a lack of concentration and too much distraction, doesn't do themselves any favors. Whether (s)he lives up to the expectations of the others is the big question on top of that.

The distinction between importance and urgency in that case follows the concept of Eisenhower, which attempts to put upcoming tasks into different categories. Here, important matters are handled first while unimportant ones are eliminated. In the last century, this theory was practiced and taught by President Dwight D. Eisenhower. All jobs are distributed into four squares according to the categories *important / not important* and *urgent / not urgent*. All tasks in the square *not important + not urgent* are not being handled at all or not personally. We will use this framework in the topic of self-confidence.

If we are personally in a stage of stable self-confidence we are more capable of saying no, setting limits and not jumping at any request. If you are deeply interested in becoming a self-confident person, you must practice these patterns of behavior as often as possible. Afterwards you will automatically feel stronger. These qualities are referred to as "psychological muscles" and just as our physical muscles grow if we train them, so do our psychological muscles. We can be sure that by setting priorities carefully we will develop a larger self-confidence and a greater self-respect.

On the other hand, if we are at a stage of our lives at which we feel insecure, we react quickly to requests or pressure from outside. We have less inner standing and we give in to demands without thinking about them. Often we don't realize at all how we treat ourselves. However, we notice when other people do so in our environment. For example, the secretary who is not able to just let the phone ring during a meeting although it had been arranged that way. Or the sales assistant in a bakery who instead of serving you gets involved in an argument with a colleague. Distraction is omnipresent, but self-confident people make decisions about priorities alone and don't let themselves be steamrolled or manipulated.

Our self-respect grows when we allow ourselves to profoundly feel what is important and how we can turn this feeling into action. Feeling profoundly means using our senses. By all means, doing this is not always possible but it is possible more often than we think at first. Even if we have a superior who swamps us over with work we can start to steadily develop an atmosphere of peacefully doing everything one by one. Saying "all-at-once" is a manipulative mechanism and it is important that we are aware of it.

In no way should we blame ourselves. We are all likely to be trapped by all of our burdens.. The boss, who wants to have many tasks handled practically at once, doesn't act that way with bad intention but more due to pragmatism. We can be happy about not having multitasked when we remain calm and settle one thing after another, perhaps even with short breaks in between.

We certainly reap the benefits when we deal more carefully with others and ourselves. That's the way life is. Although it is not that easy, we need to forget the self-perception: "I am always there for everyone, I am flexible and extremely brave, I am an easy-going and ingenious person who is never overburdened". Giving up on this self-perception may cause us to lose some security but we gain more balance and less exertion. We spare our resources. If we really want to live according to the recommendations of brain researchers, it is probably advisable at this stage to act this way. In the long run, we will be far better at settling our tasks and which boss wouldn't notice that?

## 2.7 Parents and Educators as Multitaskers

What kind of a role model would you like to be?

Multitasking is a big issue in families. Name a mother who doesn't continuously moan about all the chores that ought to be instantly settled at the same time! People with many children know all about the large amount of pending questions and issues as well as how many things that are crammed into the little time slot that is one day. Mothers and fathers certainly accomplish a lot in raising their children. They provide the important fundamentals to their children and the society. Raising children gives an inexplicable joy but the fundamental work of it is hard and parents take exerting efforts every single day.

Is it even possible to deal with our everyday lives without the act of multitasking?

At first glance, multitasking is often the only way to survive situations with children while handling everyday life. Nevertheless at this stage it is worth thinking "less is more."

Sometimes children, dependent on their age of course, only need a little of one's permanent presence. Little boys and girls ought to feel that they are important and that their parents are always there for them. Parents when they are not constantly at hand help their children to gradually learn to respect limits. Not all kids' questions have to be answered in detail immediately. It is definitely possible to put off discussions to a later point in time. Again, this is dependent on the child's age. Children feel that they are seen as important when their issues are being brought up again, especially when they are regarded as not being a distraction to mom and dad.

If you succeed in placing limits and giving yourself short – even very short - breaks, you will be more aware afterwards and you will be able to attend to the needs of your children.

Reducing multitasking in families means to gradually overburden yourself less and less, and to allow yourself to set limits and priorities. In doing so, children will learn that respecting limits is simply part of good co-existence. We will get back to that later. A final comment for now, whoever has learned to set limits and to create for themselves the necessary freedom in some areas won't, in turn, overlook important needs of others anymore but will much rather notice them automatically, which is an important goal.

## 2.8 Partnership, Friendship and Multitasking

In a partnership or friendship, it is a great gift if one dedicates undivided time and attention to the other, adapts to him, listens to him and takes notice of him. The success of therapeutic talks is primarily due to how the therapist acts towards the patient and not so much about what the therapist actually says. Experiencing complete attention, being listened to without ifs or buts and without distraction does a lot of good surprisingly often. Every human being needs attention. He who feels that he's being taken seriously and considered important and who feels that they are in the center of the focus of his counterpart has a completely different relationship than someone who only happens to be around.

How do we treat the important people in our environment? Do we continuously pay short but real attention to them? Or do we let ourselves be distracted by all sorts of things quickly? In this context, multitasking is not a skill but a serious disruption. Even if different matters lure us due to their importance, something totally different is often more important. Not the phone. Not the laundry basket. But a few minutes with another person.

This is your partner, who sits with you, your sweetheart, having tea. Actually she would love to tell you what has happened in her job. Still you only listen briefly and then talk yourself. Two unimportant monologues happen simultaneously. Even worse, you're not giving attention to her words but instead are constantly checking your e-mails and afterwards answering two calls. You've run out of things to talk about before even stirring your coffee. Or another example: we all know the hostess who apologizes for the not so perfect cake and thus stalls any important talk with her friend. These are small examples of the everyday life that constantly happen in a similar way. All in all, the outcome is not good.

## 2.9 Multitasking and Burn-out

Whoever wants to do too much at once demands too much from himself. As multitasking is still quite highly thought of in the social consensus it is always difficult to trace the source of feeling overburdened. We consider it normal that we have to complete our work and settle all sorts of things at the same time. In certain parts of gatherings in companies it may be the case such as at the reception of a hospital or in the office of the secretary, where all calls come in. However, with mindfulness and well-considered organization it would be possible in many cases to solve tasks calmly, one by one. Whoever becomes more and more aware of their style of working has the chance to optimize the senses with a beneficial slow-down. Only using multitasking as a last resort is an important burn-out-prophylaxis.

## 3. How is Multitasking Always Setting Traps?

Perhaps you have already noticed how you are overburdened by multitasking. Many of us try to counteract. Yet we don't always succeed in the way that we would wish to. Different factors account for this.

### 3.1 Contribution of the Social Environment

Throughout our social environment, multitasking is still considered a high quality. It might be easier to live in a Zen monastery in this respect but, nevertheless, an escape to an island is no solution. After all, we are surrounded by people who place demands on us. Being aware of our value and our limits, and accepting both of these is the only way to respond to our social environment. This isn't easy and we keep on failing.

### 3.2 We Want to Meet Everyone's Expectations

We are belittling ourselves every single time we give in to demands from the outside. These pressures keep us from focusing. It is important that we constantly, or as often as possible, keep an eye on our own status. Doing so means that we can freely choose whether we allow requests from the outside to keep us from our goal. It is beneficial for our notion of self-respect not to automatically and thoughtlessly deviate but only deviate when we really want to.

Some of us however would like to be everybody's darling. Being popular or appreciated by everyone can give you great attitude towards life at first. We think that it is necessary for our own self-perception to always be available and react to all requests. Immediately we inevitably fall into the multitasking trap.

The famous saying that you can't please everyone is absolutely applicable in this context. We can try as hard as we can but we will always fail to live up to the expectations of the people around us and even more so, our own. Thankfully, we always have consolatory feelings afterwards: "at least we gave our best", "we are knackered but we went the extra mile," and "we did everything in our power." Many of us dwell on this reward. But are theses feelings a desirable goal? Or do we have a different valuable purpose in life?

We don't always receive absolute admiration when we exert ourselves multi-purposefully. The people around us often feel that something is wrong with our commitment. If we don't find peace and see ourselves in the role of the all-round man/woman, our mental overload, our starving need for relaxation and enjoyment, becomes noticeable to others and weakens our charisma. When this occurs, we definitely don't get what we secretly hope for: appreciation.

## 3.3 The Urge for Distraction

Our multitasking trap plays a special role if we want to distract ourselves. Perhaps we are at a particular stage of our life in which we just want to be showed in work so we can't think about certain things. After breakups or after disappointing experiences many people react accordingly and for the transitional period distraction can be a useful tool to calm our psyche. It can make us more capable of enduring a grievous situation. On the other hand, if multitasking becomes a lifestyle, if it lasts for months and then years, the danger becomes imminent. It can become an urge to let oneself be smothered by and loaded with work. Due to that it is impossible to tackle your real matters and commitments. The lifestyle of "too much" can last for years and even decades. It can become a constant in our lives.

At first we often receive admiration and praise, when we seem fairly omnipotent and energetic. However, this reward has been collected at a high cost. In the long run, mental overload and repression generally appear in physical pain or in symptoms similar to those of depression due to exertion, burn-out or vegetative dystonia.

## 3.4 Outside Control vs. Inside Control

That we often can't make do without multitasking is also owing to the fact that we are so used to allowing ourselves to be controlled from outside. Advertisement and media contribute to a great extent to us being overwhelmed by allurements and offers of consumption. Actually going for these things is, of course, in our control. After all, we are not being forced to do anything. Yet we are constantly being manipulated. Fascinating advertisement fliers, and commercial clips, "unbelievable" special offers, countless free time and consumption opportunities don't leave us unmoved but trigger demands. It is indeed difficult to resist such a huge amount of temptations. We can succeed if we manage to counteract with the help of our own, stable standing. Some people are blessed with such a standing, perhaps due to the fact that they have grown up in an environment in which setting priorities was consistently practiced. Most of us, though, are forced to work out a considerate mindfulness and a protection against allurements. This also includes being aware of manipulations in advertising.

## 4. The Discovery of Mindfulness and Awareness

Is there a solution? Are there possibilities of walking one's life with consciousness and without being influenced from outside? The notion of a mindful and aware lifestyle points in a hopeful direction.

## 4.1 What Does Mindfulness Mean? A Pleasant Reward!

Mindfulness is a lifestyle, which brings us together with the most interesting person - ourselves.

Those who live mindfully enjoy the here and now. Neither the past nor the future dominate. The very moment counts. Due to that, the past proves to be profound and precious. Those who don't think about the future when they're in the present and do not allow themselves to be distracted by current impulses are able to achieve a life with a high intensity and high standard.

People that are settled experience true joy and can calmly endure suffering. They can do a lot for themselves and others. Those that are in touch with themselves, ignore pressure from the outside, and are controlled are able to have short or long breaks whenever they need them. When you have achieved this you will be able to face other issues. If you learn not to be controlled by your environment but attain consideration and mindfulness for yourself, you will also be able to be considerate and mindful to those around you. Unfortunately no matter how hard we try, we can only have relationships with others once we become one with ourselves.

This description sounds like it's very close to ideal. Most of us will approach this lifestyle but won't completely reach it. Perfection is by all means not the goal. Yet, he who moves into that direction will feel positive changes, at first on himself but after a while, he can tell it by the way people react.

Anyway, what is the reward of this new and considerate way of life?

## 4.2 Self-efficacy Increases

Just like multitasking weakens our self-perception in the long run, a considerate attitude strengthens us and fuels our self-confidence. The more we feel that we are the rulers of our own personal kingdoms, the more we confirm our own value. Moreover, the stronger our self-esteem becomes the easier it will be for us to preserve our standing and to listen to our inner voice. If we leave the multitasking lifestyle and move to more mindfulness and increased consideration, we will move into a direction that makes us grow. At first we feel it in ourselves, but later others will feel it as well. We will be taken more seriously, we will be less abused for all sorts of actions, and we will gain time for more important things.

## 4.3 Relationship of Couples and Mindfulness

Attention and consideration is a vital elixir for relationships. He who is aware of himself can communicate more clearly. He who can allow his needs to himself is much more capable of allowing needs to his counterpart. Not all wishes and desires can and should be fulfilled. Hence, feeling them and not instantly judging them is a good way of dealing with impulses. Deciding afterwards, as the ruler of yourself, will give clarity in determining what is to happen with the wishes, whether they ought to be deliberately pursued or responsibly put aside. That way, many types of repression become unnecessary.

He who treats other people with consideration also perceives with differentiation but doesn't impose anything onto others. He respects limits and the specific qualities of his counterparts. These skills are treasures in every relationship.

The attention we dedicate to our companion or our friends is a big gift. We grant it voluntarily. We can also legitimately refuse it. In that case it would be best served with a short explanation for transparency and trust. We can also limit attention temporarily. It is very likely that we sometimes have to do it. It's all about developing a sense for the essential. Not necessarily throughout day and night but from time to time in shorter or longer sequences, keeping up the quality of mutual attention is the secret of good relationships.

By the way, all bosses who strive for a good leadership are welcome to make use of this advice. Even short conversations or conduct meetings with a high degree of attention may create within merely a few minutes a counterpart who values himself and feels that he's being taken seriously.

## 4.4 Mindfulness and Upbringing

The things important in relationships are also valid in the raising of children. Kids appreciate when we take them seriously, when we listen to them and when we have time for them. A part of the day in which we give our children full attention, consideration and affection is more important than many little pieces of answers throughout the whole day. If children feel that we are not always available but that we always dedicate full moments without distraction to them, then it will strengthen their state of mind and their self-esteem. Parents and educators who treat their children mindfully also do not try to manipulate them or impose their own needs on them. Respecting limits is part of being conscious and fair when dealing with people. Regardless of whether children or adults, the elderly or youngsters, everybody loves being respected. Mutual respect strengthens relationships.

Mindfulness concerning upbringing means that we as educators have to sharpen our senses. It means that we must take care of the needs of the people under our care. Those who are constantly in touch with themselves are more aware that something concerns their children and that they might need something important. One can inquire about problems well by speaking not too condescendingly or being patronizing but rather by mindfully listening and by being seriously interested in what our children have to say.

## 4.5 Mindfulness and the Workplace

Mindfulness in the job can have similar consequences as it can in our private lives. We take the liberty and time to listen properly, we don't try to help thoughtlessly, but we set priorities. We take the time to settle tasks one by one and we only expect multitasking from others under exceptional circumstances. It could be that we become more successful using this style of work in the long run. At least it is far more sustainable than doing everything all at once. Mindfulness at work also means that we feel our limits, that we respect, and constantly remind ourselves of them. Regular breaks are an important fundamental for a burn-out-prophylaxis. We need to adhere to this imperatively, if we care for ourselves.

## 4.6 Anecdote About Mindfulness

An ancient parable about the issue of mindfulness dates back - according to the oral tradition - to an Asian Zen monk. It nicely illustrates in few words what mindfulness is all about:

*Once upon a time a man was being asked how he could be so happy despite his numerous engagements and tasks. He said:*
*"When I stand, I stand,*
*When I go, I go,*
*When I sit, I sit,*
*When I eat, I eat,*
*When I love, I love..."*

*Then his questioners butted in and said:*
*"We do that to, but what do you do beyond that?"*
*Again he said:*
*"When I stand, I stand,*
*When I go, I go,*
*When I..."*
*Again the people said:*
*"But we do that, too!"*
*Yet he said to them:*
*"No - when you sit, you already stand.*
*When you stand, you already run,*
*When you run, you have already reached your goal."*

Perhaps to you this little story can be the same as it is to me: a profound image. If you are under the weight of stress in your everyday life, of hectic living and of multitasking but you feel that you should go a different way, think of this story.

# 5. How Do We Cultivate Mindfulness and Self-awareness?

## 5.1 Sharpening Self-perception

The first step is to get to know yourself better. In doing so discover your own journey. There are different ways. The first condition and an important component is that we take time off for ourselves, simply having a few hours of free time without commitments, without pressure, without work.

This thought scares some of us. For people that aren't used to being by themselves, not having tasks at hand, a daunting void opens up. Sometimes it can be helpful to recall joyful childhood moments for inspiration on what to do in our free time. Examples include wandering through fields, woods, and meadows, creating imaginative portraits, singing, modeling with clay or simply lying in the grass. All of these pleasures await those who do them. When you are doing nothing and enjoying it often completely new thoughts appear, a feeling of awareness about oneself as a unique creature is being created. It is not about achieving or creating. It's merely about enjoying, experiencing and drifting.

We can also train mindfulness in the presence of others, in Yoga-classes or in the context of meditation. In yoga, there are moments in which you analyze yourself, for example the glance at the mirror in order to perceive the eyes consciously as well as the completely unique coloring of the pupils. These are the very moments, in which we are very close to ourselves and that makes our mindfulness grow.

## 5.2 Gaining Insight, Changing Behaviors

He who changes his behavior often accomplishes a lot in doing so. After an "aha-effect", during which we gain important insights, we sometimes change our attitude quickly and easily.

However, afterwards we almost always try to consolidate this new behavior and move according to its direction.

## 5.3 Visualizing the Goal

As far as the topic of multitasking versus mindfulness is concerned, we can steadily recall our goal through principles or pictures. Which word or image do you take with you, what keeps on reminding you of the direction that you are moving in? Is it the empowering image of being your own ruler inspiring you to work out a standing and to settle things one by one by setting priorities? Or is it the famous and silly image of the Swiss Army knife, which scares you off continuing to live your individual multitasking style? Could it be the "hamster in the wheel" confronting you with your never-ending efforts? Does the image of the lion peacefully sprawling under the sun, help you?

You can put together your own desired image in your thoughts where you can always recall it. You can also paint your own picture or design a poster by using a collage. It is important that the work of art contains your own individual key issues since you are a unique original and you let yourself be motived by your own colorful goals.

## 5.4 Little exercises for Mindfulness: Getting to the Here and Now

Perhaps you can recognize the state in which your thoughts circulate through your head and you can't escape? Past things grieve you and you worry about the future. Often these are very specific fears that we can't repress. Often these thoughts spiral out of control since we predict all kinds of theoretical catastrophes and horror scenarios that could happen. The following exercise can help you get back to the present and relax.

**Step 1:** Try to mentally absorb what you are seeing at the moment. Try to peacefully name and describe three objects, one by one. Perhaps you see the clouds in the sky, your shopping basket and your trainers - describe these things to yourself.

**Step 2:** Try to absorb everything you are hearing at the moment. Describe three sounds. Perhaps you hear the wind howling, the computer humming, the birds chirping, and the silence. Whatever there is for your ears to perceive: name and describe it to yourself.

**Step 3:** What are you feeling at the moment? The fabric of the chair you're sitting in? The chill in the air or the soft carpet? Take your time to sense these things. Name and describe the impressions to yourself.

After this exercise, you will be feeling more relaxed and calm. You have arrived in the "now." Try it and afterwards you will be ready for solution-solving actions. Maybe you will also be in the mood to just chill out and allow yourself a nice treat.

**Another exercise is** to play your favorite song when being at home, ideally by yourself, and to let your body freely follow the rhythm of the music. In doing so, you will learn to completely lay back and relax. Don't hesitate to close the curtains, you will feel more comfortable knowing that you are unobserved. If possible, listen to music through loudspeakers and not through headphones, as this doesn't restrict your freedom as much. You are definitely allowed loud music if you want it! Which kind of music you choose is up to you and your mood. Classic may stimulate you, dance triggers rhythmic movements and love songs perhaps make you tremble. It doesn't matter what and how. Just give it a try.

**A Madame Missou secret tip:** The mindfulness App of Mind-Apps. You can buy it on iTunes, in the Google Play Store at

Amazon. The application is a tool to increase the presence and mindfulness in your life. It helps you practice the difficult aspect of mindfulness - which is to remind yourself to be mindful. The App includes guided meditations, silent meditations and sound imitations, mindfulness memories and so on, and so on... The convenience about the App is that you can always have it with you on your cell phone. Whether you are at the office, on the train or at home you can always spontaneously practice in 5-, 10-, 20-, 30-, or even in 60-minute sessions.

## 6. Excursion: Enjoyment Provides Profoundness and Laughing is Healthy

As we know, laughing is pure medicine for your spirit, soul and body. Where does this beneficial effect come from?

The reason lies in the fact that we are ourselves when laughing. If we laugh sincerely, we really don't do anything else in that moment. We are completely at one with ourselves. We think about nothing else, we enjoy the moment and let other thoughts and feelings go. Letting go completely sometimes only takes seconds but you know from your own experience that you can burst into laughter for several minutes. This laughter clearly means, "I am letting go." We forget our fears, worries and annoyances and even our pain for a short time. That way we have a wonderful way to deeply relax.

What is true for laughter is also relevant for other enjoyments. Enjoying is completely different from consuming. Consuming aims at quantity, enjoyments at quality. Who can enjoy experiences and profoundness? Whether it's about good food, sexuality, music, about art or natural experiences, whoever is capable of letting go, sets oneself free from demands and outside control.

True enjoyment generally excludes multitasking though. He who manages tasks like a juggler manages balls, runs in a wheel like a hamster, or operates in all directions cannot reach a level of profoundness as he is constantly being distracted. That means that we only really get to profound enjoyment once we get out of the multitasking mode.

In this context, the wonderful anecdote *"Anecdote to the Decline of the Work Ethics"* from the year 1963 by Heinrich Böll ought to be mentioned. The little story is about an overeager tourist and a deeply relaxed fisherman in Southern Europe, both of whom are being involved in a discussion about work ethics. The humbly dressed fisherman is being woken up by the clicking noise of the tourist's photo camera. The tourist asks the fisherman what he was doing at the beach, and why he wasn't out on the sea fishing. After all, today was a splendid day in order to get a great catch and there were many fish outside. After some hesitation, the fisherman answers calmly that today he had already been out there and caught so well that it was still enough for the following days. The tourist replied that the fisherman could go out again another two, three or four times and then set up his own enterprise, then a bigger enterprise. This growth would steadily increase, until he could even deliver his fish abroad. The tourist is being carried away by an eager craze and strives for even more superlatives. At the end the fisherman could have earned enough in order to only sit at the port and to relax in peace. The fisher responds that he was already doing just that: sitting at the port and relaxing. A little envious, the tourist walks off.

So much about the topic enjoyment and mindfulness…

## 7. Summary

Multitasking is tiring and uses a lot of our energy. When we are mindful and considerate on the other hand, we as well as our fellow humans benefit. By striving for mindfulness we learn to treat our entire lives with care accordingly. We find it easier to treat the people in our environment as well as ourselves gently.

The great thing about this way of living is that with every step we gain real treasures. We find our precious inner balance, we develop a real self-confidence and we experience the incredibly satisfying feeling of self-worth.

I truly believe that that's what life is actually all about.

All right, we have made it. The first 45-minute guidebook about mindfulness is completed. If you have read this book carefully, calmly, steadily and without distraction, then congratulations! If you haven't quite succeeded and put the book aside from time to time, then it is by all means no failure. Practice makes perfect, and nobody was born this way. From now on, keep on practicing your mindfulness like a muscle. You will be grateful to yourself for it!

I hope that you have discovered interesting suggestions for your own situation in this little, introductive guide. Perhaps you can take some of the ideas with you and make them a part of your everyday life. Try out the lifestyle based on mindfulness in small steps.

Perhaps you are indeed more advanced in this area and you have received a few new initiatives. In any case, I hope you will move on successfully in the process of inner mindfulness.

*Bisous,*

*Madame Missou* (who is grateful for your **reviews on Amazon**, 2-3 lines are absolutely enough!)

## Similar books of the author you might like:

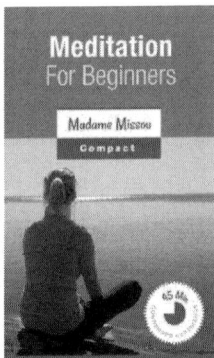

# 7. Appendices

## How Did You like this Book?

*"No feedback is good feedback"* – this small proverb is very prevalent throughout most Internet businesses. But a small compliment or praise doesn't cost the sender much, but means so much to the receiver. If you liked my little guide and you feel like that it helped you, I would be more than ecstatic about your review on amazon. Of course, any feedback is welcome (though I like positive feedback especially well ;-) ). Both kinds of feedback help me to continuously improve and extend this little guide. So please just spend one or two minutes of your time on feedback about the book on amazon.com – **I am thankful!**

## About the Author Madame Missou

I was born 1960 in Bamako (Mali). My father was a French ambassador, my mother worked as an Argentinian botanist. I studied art and art history at the Université Paris-Sorbonne. At the age of 25, I moved out into the new world. I established the gallery *"Madame Missou's Best World Arts"* and played parts in many different musicals. At the beginning of the 90s, I sold my gallery and moved back to Europe. Before settling in Berlin in 1999, I moved around quite a bit spending considerable amounts of time in Lisbon, Copenhagen, Moscow and London. Here in Germany, I've been happily and quietly living with my family for the past 16 years. My experience allows me to work as a writer, life coach, consultant, and artist. I have already published numerous bestselling guides in German, mostly about typical topics involving women. Including this one that you are holding in your hands right now!

If you want to find out more about me, feel free to visit my website   www.MadameMissou.com,   my   facebook   page

## Legalities and Imprint

*Madame Missou is represented by the*

Maracuja GmbH
Laerheider Weg 13
47669 Wachtendonk
info@madamemissou.com
*Translation by Paul Wesendonk, herr-paul-consulting.com*
*Cover design by Claudia Braun, extenso.de*
*Copyright Cover: kk75, photocase.com*

18004826R00022

Printed in Great Britain
by Amazon